When God Sent Me to Hell

Dr Michael H Yeager

Copyright © 2018 Dr Michael H Yeager

All rights reserved.

ISBN: 9781727467093

All rights reserved. No part of this book is allowed to be reproduced, stored in a retrieval system, or transmitted by any form or by any means-electronic, mechanical, photocopy, recording, or otherwise-without prior written permission of the copyright owner, except by a reviewer who wishes to quote brief passages in connection with a review for inclusion in a magazine, website, newspaper, podcast, or broadcast. All Scripture quotations, unless otherwise indicated, are taken from the King James Authorized Version of the Bible.

CONTENTS

CHAPTER ONE

*Now I was stationed on an island in the Navy in the Aleutian chain on an island called Adak, Alaska, which is known for its many earth quakes. This island is where I was stationed in the military as an electrician's mate third class. The Navy base had a top-secret military installation and was used as a harbor for submarines and ships.

The top-secret installation was so hush-hush that most of us on the base did not really know what was taking place there. When I first arrived on the base, I quickly had to get used to the tremors and continual earthquakes. There were times I experienced tremors and quakes so strong they would wake me out of my sleep. My bed would shake so violently that I thought I was going to fall out of it.

I remember one night when I first arrived I was sleeping very soundly. All of a sudden my bed not only began to shake, but it was literally bouncing up and down like a rubber ball. I thought it was the men in my barracks playing a newbie trick on me. I automatically began to yell for them to stop before I opened my eyes. But when I opened my eyes and looked around no one was there. That was how much the building shook.

My Journey to Hell Begins

Now, one night I was deep in prayer with Willy, (I had only been saved for about two months) an African American brother in my barracks. I had the privilege of seeing Willie come back to Christ. At one time, previously he had walked with the Lord but had backslid. Before and after he was saved our nickname for him was "Willy Wine" because now he was filled with new wine. As we were praying together, something very strange and very frightening began to happen to me. At the time of this event there was a gathering of some men in our battalion. They were having a party in the common area right outside our sleeping quarters where we were praying. The party they were having was quite loud with music and laughter, but it did not hinder us from crying out to God for souls.

As we were praying, I could sense that something was about to happen. The hair on the back of my arms and neck stood up on end. It was as if electricity was filling the very atmosphere around us. I sensed a strong tugging to go deeper in prayer. I gave myself completely over to the spirit of intercession, crying out to the Lord.

I began to cry out in prayer to God intensely, asking Him to allow me to have a supernatural experience of hell. I wanted this in order that I would have a greater and deeper compassion, a deeper love, a deeper understanding for the lost. I truly wanted to know the pains, the sorrows, the torments, the fears, and the agonies of those in hell. I wanted to weep and wail, to travail with a broken heart over the unconverted to reach them more effectively.

Please understand that I believe God put this desire, this prayer, into my heart for the love of souls. I began to pray in a realm that I had never been in before when suddenly an overwhelming and tangible darkness descended upon me.

"And when the sun was going down, a deep sleep fell upon Abram; and, lo, an horror of great darkness fell upon him" (Gen. 15:12).

A frightening darkness enveloped me. Everything around me disappeared. I no longer heard the music or the party that was taking place. Even though Willie was right there with me, I did not hear or see him. And it seemed as if time itself had come to a stop. To my utter shock, amazement, and horror, the floor and the building around me began to shake more violently than I had ever experienced before. Usually when we did get a quake (Adak Alaska) it would only last a matter of seconds. But in this situation the shaking did not stop as it normally did, rather it increased.

The Floor of the Building Ripped Open

All I could do at this moment was to try to hug the floor and hang on for dear life. The darkness lifted, but I could not see Willie anywhere. Then a terrible ripping and grinding noise filled the air. I saw the floor of the barracks ripple like that of a wave on the sea. The very floor of the barracks that I was laying upon began to tear and rip apart. I watched in stunned amazement and horror as the floor tiles popped and stretched. The concrete and steel within the building began to twist and rip apart. And the floor I was laying on began to split and tear open right below me.

I immediately began to look for a way to get out of the building. Everything was shaking so violently that I could not get up off the floor to make a dash to escape. The dust and dirt in the room was so thick and heavy that I could hardly breathe. Now this rip in the floor began to enlarge and became an opening. I would call it more like a hole. I began to slip and fall into this hole; I tried desperately to reach for any kind of handhold that I could find. I began to scream and yell for help. But there was no one to help me. I became increasingly desperate trying to grab hold of something, anything that I could get my hands on. Objects around me began to fall through this hole in the floor. I watched as physical objects slipped past me into this hole. And I could feel myself sliding more and more.

No matter how desperately I was trying to cling to and hold on to items to prevent my falling, there was nothing that I could do. Finally, I slipped and fell backward as if falling off a ladder. As I was falling, everything seemed to go into slow motion like film that is slowed for a preview. I was falling with parts of the crumbling building all around me. I watched as I fell past twisted steel beams, concrete floors, walls ripped into pieces, plumbing, and heating pipes, and sparking electric wires. I went past the underground tunnels that connected the buildings together.

The next thing that I knew I was falling past the ground and rock of the island. This terrible rip in the earth, this hole that I was falling down began to take on the form and similarity of that of a well, like an endless tube, an ever- proceeding pit. It became approximately three feet wide. As I was falling, I was desperately trying to grab hold of the rocks that were protruding from the sides of this deep dark pit, but my descent was too fast. None of the rocks seemed to protrude far enough for me to get a good handhold.

Even as I was falling down this hole I was not experiencing any fear of going to hell or fear of dying because I had a calm assurance that I knew my heart was right with God. I was ready to meet my Savior. Don't misunderstand; I am not saying that I had no fear! Though I knew in my heart that I was right with God, I was still filled with the absolute horror of not knowing what was happening to me. At that moment I did not have any idea whatsoever that I was plunging into hell.

I kept trying to figure out how I could stop my descent into this hole. What I was experiencing was mind- boggling because to me it was truly physically happening. I could feel, touch, smell, hear, and see everything that was happening to me. Actually everything seemed to be amplified beyond my normal five senses.

Through the years I had experienced dreams, nightmares, and hallucinations from drugs and alcohol which I had taken, but none of them came anywhere near to what I was experiencing at that very moment. My mind kept screaming, How can I stop my descent into this hole? I just kept on falling down and down into this really deep dark hole. Deeper and deeper I fell—down, down, down. I must have fallen mile after mile.

"He hath said, which heard the words of God, which saw the vision of the Almighty, falling into a trance, but having his eyes open" (Num. 24:4).

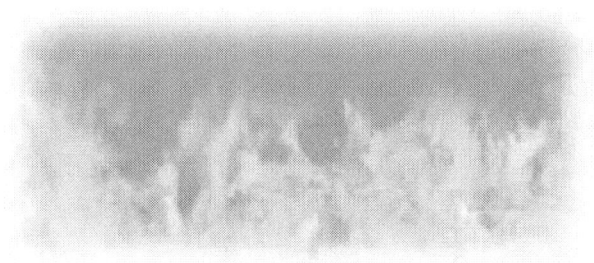

CHAPTER TWO

Terrible Stink of Hell

Now as I was falling down this deep dark hole, a violent and overwhelming hot wind began blowing from somewhere at the bottom of this shaft and hitting me in the face. It was a suffocating, nauseating, stinking wind. It smelled of rotting eggs and sulfur. It became almost impossible for me to breathe. I tried to use my shirt as a mask to filter out the stinking smell. But it was to no avail.

"Their slain also shall be cast out, and their stink shall come up out of their carcases, and the mountains shall be melted with their blood" (Isa. 34:3).

Actually this experience in and of itself should have been enough to kill me. I kept trying to get a breath of fresh air, but there was none to be had. As I was desperately trying to breathe I continued to fall. How long I fell down this hole I do not know. But it seemed to me to have no end, to be bottomless. Or was it? As I looked down in the direction that I was falling feet first, I looked between my feet. I began to see a very small and very faint orange, yellowish, reddish glow. It began extremely small, but as I continued to fall toward the light it became brighter and brighter.

Never-Ending Cavern of Hell

Before I knew it I was out of this black hole, this tunnel. I had entered into a humongous and gigantic, seemingly never-ending cavern. I could see no end in sight. It was as if I had fallen into a whole different world, an underworld. I was falling like a skydiver. Now, I was tens of thousands of feet above an ocean of liquefied, swirling lava and blazing fire.

Thousands of feet below me was a frightening, boiling lake of fire. It was burning, churning, and bubbling, almost similar to that of a pan of overheated boiling molasses on a stove. I could see that it was extremely aggravated and violent. It was almost as if it was filled and possessed with an aggressive, living fury. Fire and brimstone were exploding upon its surface in every direction sending flames rising thousands of feet into the air.

The flames darted here and there like a huge blazing gasoline fire. It would appear one moment in one area, vanish, and then appear somewhere else. At the same time there were air- shattering explosions, like volcanoes erupting across this vast surface of liquefied lava. It was like a living, swirling, obsessed whirlpool of fire, brimstone, and lava. It glowed different colors of red, orange, and yellow.

Perhaps a better description would be that it pulsated and radiated like hot charcoal in a furnace, with molten steel, liquefied stone, and swirling gases. Fire danced across the top of its surface like miniature tornadoes spinning violently out of control. They would spin until they ascended up into the black nothingness of the cavern I was falling in.

Intense Heat in Hell

As I continued to descend toward the surface of this ocean, this endless lake of liquid fire and lava. It seemed to me that I was about ten thousand feet above the surface of this ocean. And even at ten thousand feet, the heat that was hitting me was so intense that my very flesh felt as if it was withering, melting, and burning. It felt as if it was being ripped off of my hands, my face, and my body. In the past I have received minor burns whether it was from cooking or from building a fire to keep the house warm. But that was minor—a mosquito bite compared to what was happening to me now.

As I looked at my skin and flesh it was beginning to bubble and blister. My whole body was beginning to burn. My clothes were catching on fire, and I could not put them out. My shoes were melting to my feet. My hair caught on fire like the wick on a candlestick. It was as if someone had doused me with gasoline and then threw a match on me. I began to scream like a madman.

At the beginning of this book, I asked how could anyone truly have experienced what I am sharing with you and yet not be shaken to the very core of their being every time they retell their story? I'm telling you that as I recount to you what transpired, my heart is filled with dread and trembling. At that same time my lungs felt like they were going to be burned out of my chest. I needed cool fresh air, but there was none to be had. Can you imagine what it would be like to be roasted alive slowly over an open burning pit with red hot coals? This is what I was experiencing.

Dreadful Screams of Hell

In the midst of this overwhelming pain and agony, my ears began to be filled with a strange, eerie sound—a humming sound, like a throbbing deep, moan that never stopped. As I was falling closer and closer to the surface of the burning lava, this humming, groaning, moaning sound increased in its intensity. It became an ear-piercing, overwhelming, never- ending sound that grew louder and louder. It was as if my head was surrounded by a huge hive of angry bees. As I continued to fall toward this churning, massive ocean, the sound that I was hearing became more distinct and clear. It contained ear-piercing highs and incredible heartbreaking lows with many other pitches in between that are too numerous to describe to you.

I remember asking myself in my pain and torment, "What in the world can this sound be that I am hearing? What could be causing such terrible heart wrenching, horror-filled sounds?" And then at that very moment I believe that the Spirit of the Lord opened up my understanding to what was happening to me. It hit me like an eighteen-wheel truck slamming into my body.

The sound that I was hearing was not coming from equipment, machinery or something from nature. But it was coming from human beings, my friend. The sound that was coming to my ears was from human beings who were screaming, wailing, groaning, and moaning with an incredible, intense, overwhelming pain. They were in unbelievable agony with unbearable torments. My ears were filled with the terrible screams of damned souls.

"Therefore I will wail and howl, I will go stripped and naked" (Mic. 1:8).

"And shall cast them into a furnace of fire: there shall be wailing and gnashing of teeth"(Matt. 13:42).

I remember my whole body began to shake violently almost as if I were having convulsions. It was like rivers of absolute dismay and complete horror. The bitter lamentations of suffering humanity engulfed me. Oh how their sorrows flooded my very being. Even as I retell this story to you it is as if my heart is being ripped out of my chest. And the agony and pain that I am experiencing right now is nothing compared to the agony that God is experiencing. You see, it is His will that none should perish. But all should have eternal life.

Headed to Hell

I had not understood or realized what was really happening to me. The Spirit of God must have been keeping my mind and heart blind to what was happening in order that it might create a greater impact upon my life. But now, at this very moment and second with a mind-numbing shock, I realized that God had heard my prayers. God had, for some strange reason, answered my cry quite literally. There was no turning back. There was no stopping what had begun. At the terminal velocity of124 miles an hour I was headed straight for the unbelievable torments and sufferings of hell—the terrible lake of fire which was right below me.

"And the smoke of their torment ascendeth up for ever and ever: and they have no rest day or night" (Rev. 14:11).

"If anyone's name was not found in the book of life, he was thrown into the lake of fire" (Rev. 20:15).

"Therefore hell hath enlarged herself, and opened up her mouth without measure: and their glory, and their multitude, and their pomp, and he that rejoiceth, shall descend into it" (Isa. 5:14).

Hell is not a respecter of people—of gender, color, race, position, wealth, or education. You see, my friend, Jesus Christ spoke a lot about hell. Jesus spoke on hell ten times more than He did about heaven. Who is Jesus Christ to the believer? He is our everything, our very life and breath, our all in all. He is the foundation upon which we build our very existence. All of our eternal and immortal hopes are placed upon Him.

"And are built upon the foundation of the apostles and prophets, Jesus Christ himself being the chief corner stone" (Eph. 2:20).

"Neither is there salvation in any other: for there is none other name under heaven given among men, whereby we must be saved" (Acts 4:12).

"When Christ, who is our life, shall appear, then shall ye also appear with him in glory" (Col. 3:4).

The words of Christ must take complete and absolute superiority over all else! It really doesn't matter who proclaims or declares that there is no hell. For Jesus Christ, our Lord and Master, the author and finisher of our salvation, declares otherwise. Look at what Jesus declared in the gospels:

"And if thy right eye offend thee, pluck it out, and cast it from thee: for it is profitable for thee that one of thy members should perish, and not that thy

whole body should be cast into hell. And if thy right hand offend thee, cut it off, and cast it from thee: for it is profitable for thee that one of thy members should perish, and not that thy whole body should be cast into hell"(Matt. 5:29-30).

"But the children of the kingdom shall be cast out into outer darkness: there shall be weeping and gnashing of teeth" (Matt. 8:12).

"The Son of man shall send forth his angels, and they shall gather out of his kingdom all things that offend, and them which do iniquity; And shall cast them into a furnace of fire: there shall be wailing and gnashing of teeth" (Matt. 13:41-42).

My friends, please listen to me, hell is real. The Bible says that hell is:

•**A great fire**

•**A fierce fire**

•**An irresistible fire**

•**A continual fire**

•**A dark fire**

•**An unquenchable fire**

•**An everlasting fire**

CHAPTER THREE
Why People Are in Hell

People are in hell because of rebellion and disobedience to God. It is what the Bible calls sin. And what is sin? It is when you live by the standard of this: Not God's will be done, but my will be done. It is living a self- centered life, which is the gateway to hell.

It is the broad and wide path that leads men to eternal damnation, to separation from God where there is never-ending anguish, unutterable sorrows, everlasting pain, and eternal torments.

"Enter ye in at the strait gate: for wide is the gate, and broad is the way, that leadeth to destruction, and many there be which go in thereat" (Matt. 7:13).

Sin is being self-pleasing, self-loving, self-obsessed, self-centered, self-serving, and self-seeking. It is the vain pursuit of ungodly pleasures. Sin is rebellion and mutiny, and disobedience to

God and His holy Word. It is that which is contrary to God's divine nature and His character, spitting in the very face of the One who died for us and gave Himself for us. Those in sin make themselves god, sitting upon the throne of their own heart with no pursuit of the Father's will.

I beg you with all the sincerity of my heart that if you do not know Jesus Christ in a personal, intimate way, please turn to Christ right now and come out of your sins. Turn from your self-pleasing and wicked ways. Please change your mind, and give Jesus your heart, soul, life, mind, and body. We need to give all of our selves to Jesus, even as He gave all of Himself for us! Jesus, by His own divine nature, will give you complete and total victory over the satanic nature.

"Whereby are given unto us exceeding great and precious promises: that by these ye might be partakers of the divine nature, having escaped the corruption that is in the world through lust" (2 Pet. 1:4).

You see God became a man and gave Himself as the ultimate sacrifice for our sins. Thereby providing the victory we need to overcome the world, flesh, and the devil.

"For this purpose the Son of God was manifested, that he might destroy the works of the devil" (1 John 3:8).

He died to save our souls and to resurrect and create His divine image and nature into our hearts once again. We must determine in our hearts to give Him all that we are, all that we have, and all that we will ever be. We have borne the image of the earthly fallen Adam. Now we must bear the image of the heavenly Adam. Beloved, are you walking on the broad and wide way of sin, which leads to eternal destruction? Or are you walking on the straight and narrow pathway of loving God, loving holiness, loving faith, and loving obedience?

"The wicked shall be turned into hell, and all the nations that forget God" (Ps. 9:17).

"The way of life is above to the wise, that he may depart from hell beneath" (Prov. 15:24).

You see, my friend, we will all someday die. It does not matter who you are or what you possess. You and I will die.

"For what is your life? It is even a vapour, that appeareth for a little time, and then vanisheth away" (James 4:14).

Now here I am, God has heard my prayer, and I am falling toward the lake of fire, the ocean of damnation, at over 124 miles an hour.

Like Bobbing Corks in Hell

At about two thousand feet above the surface of the ocean of hell, the pain that was hitting my body was over whelming, unbearable, unbelievable, and all consuming. My lungs were on fire. My eyes felt like they were being burned out of my sockets. My clothes had burned and melted to my flesh. I was beyond third-degree burns.

And yet, incredibly I was still fully aware of everything that was transpiring around me. If anything, my five senses were more alive than ever before. I believe that God must have supernaturally increased my capacity to experience all that I was going through.

I was looking down in the direction in which I was headed. I could see upon the surface of the lake of fire what looked like little black objects violently bobbing up and down like fishing corks in the orange and red glow of the burning, churning, bubbling ocean of hell. As my eyes became more focused (by the grace of God), I could see thousands upon tens of thousands of these objects dotting the surface. They were everywhere. As I looked upon them, I found myself possessed by an overwhelming curiosity. I lost interest in everything else that was happening to me.

Even though I was experiencing tremendous and unbelievable pain and agony, I was still able to focus my mind and attention upon these objects. My mind was very clear and sharp. The only way to describe my curiosity was that it was supernatural. This curiosity gripped my mind and heart. And as I fell closer and closer, I could see that these objects were actually oblong, not round as I had thought. But they contained limbs at both ends. And these limbs were waving back and forth, back and forth, in a frantic jerking type of motion.

Out of my innermost being, I let out a deep, tormented groan as I suddenly realized what I was looking at. These black, bobbing objects were nothing less than human beings! People! They were masses of humanity from every nation, culture, tribe, and tongue. And they were screaming, moaning, and yelling as they were being turned and tossed about, head over heels, carried along in the swirling lava of the burning, churning, undercurrents of hell.

Now, in my past I have heard people weeping and wailing, crying over the death of a precious loved one. I have experienced this myself when our four-and-a- half-year-old little girl, Naomi, died. That same year my mother died. I wailed and wept and cried. But never had I heard crying like this, such agony, such screaming, such sorrow.

The wailing and howls of pain broke my heart. It still breaks my heart to this day as I think upon this experience. I could not tell by looking upon these burning blackened masses of humanity who or what they were. It was only by the Spirit of God that I discern these truths. For when their physical body hit the flaming fires of hell they lost their sexuality. They lost their nationality, their race and color of skin. No longer could you determine what their age was. For hell makes all people equal.

Dreadful Screams of Hell

These are souls forever damned. These are souls with no hope, escape, help, or relief from pain. Maybe these are people you and I have known—dads and moms, brothers and sisters, aunts and uncles, neighbors and friends who have died without loving Christ. Their hearts were full of the cares and lusts of this world. Their lives were full of selfishness and sin. They had no time for God or His Word. They spent their lives pursuing the useless pleasures of this world, filling their minds with vain and useless amusements, foolish entertainment, ungodly movies, involving themselves in immoral activities. The Apostle Paul warned us:

"Know this also, that in the last days perilous times shall come" (2 Tim. 3:1).

Because God is a righteous God, He must judge sin. By the time that these people discovered this truth it was too late. For they died and woke up in a dreadful, boiling lake of brimstone, sulfur, and fire. They have no way of escape, no relief from pain, and no hope for the future. These people have nothing to look forward to except endless torment, loneliness, and pain. Their bodies burned black like burnt chicken that had been overcooked on a barbecue pit. The unquenchable flames of a never-ending hell blackened their souls. Those down there looked like living and moving pieces of charcoal.

Into the Lava of Hell

Because I was so caught-up in the stark reality of what was going on before me, I did not realize that I was still falling closer and closer to the surface of the lake of fire. Suddenly, I plunged into the lava. It was like burning mud and quicksand. Immediately it sucked me in with a frightening ferocity. It engulfed me, pulling me down, swallowing me up in its hideous stomach of endless suffering and pain.

It covered me over and filled my mouth and my nose, ears and my eyes with an overwhelming, intense burning pain. The flaming sulfur of hell came into my mouth. It went down my throat, into my stomach, and filled my lungs. I was immersed in a baptism of absolute horror. My eyes felt like they were being consumed out of my sockets. And yet they were still there. My whole body was on fire and burning like a marshmallow dropped into the red coals of a campfire.

I came to the absolute bleak truth that in no way could hell ever be exaggerated. Everything I had ever heard or read about the eternal destiny of the lost and the damned, those who do not love God, does not sufficiently describe what I was experiencing right at that moment. No words could exist to describe the intense pain, the heart wrenching sorrow, the absolute agony, and the everlasting torments of hell. Hell is totally deaf to the cries and agonies of those who are swallowed up and wallowing in its belly.

"And death and hell were cast into the lake of fire. This is the second death. And whosoever was not found written in the book of life was cast into the lake of fire" (Rev. 20:14-15).

CHAPTER FOUR

Why Forever in Hell?

Over and over God has warned humanity about hell. Why? Because He does not want us to go there. He has done everything He can to save, redeem, deliver, rescue, and convert us. God longs to help us, so desperate that He gave His only begotten Son in order to rescue and save us. He took upon Himself our sins, torments, and pains.

"For God so loved the world, that he gave his only begotten Son, that whosoever believeth in him should not perish, but have everlasting life" (John 3:16).

Swallowed Up in the Darkness of Hell

Now at that very moment excruciating pain overtook me. It penetrated my mind, and inflamed every fiber of my being. It stuck to my flesh like melted black tar. The lava was like burning mud that sucked me into the very depths of hell. Deeper and deeper I sunk. It pulled me down like a whirlpool. I wish I could be more graphic in how it felt. How deep I sunk I do not know. The depths of the oceans of this present world are nothing in comparison with the depths of hell. For it is called the bottomless pit. I could not resist its current. It pulled and sucked at me like quicksand. I gave up all hope of ever coming to the surface. I was covered and engulfed in total darkness. I could not see anything. Now you understand that my eyes were not burned out of my head. I could still see. And yet I could not see, because there was no light.

The Bible declares that there is no light in hell to be had. There is no light of the sun, the moon, the stars, or even a flame. It is the darkness of eternal midnight. When I began this journey, and throughout it, for the most part I could see what was taking place. God allowed me to see because He wanted me to behold what was happening in the underworld of the lost. For those who are eternally lost in hell this is not normal. They will never see light again because they have rejected the light of Jesus Christ. They will never have the privilege of seeing the glorious lights of creation again.

"But the children of the kingdom shall be cast out into utter darkness: there shall be weeping and gnashing of teeth" (Matt. 8:12).

Can Not Die in Hell

Now, as I was sucked deeper into the lava, brimstone and sulfur, the burning mud of hell was in my mouth, and I could not breathe. My lungs were collapsing. I kept trying to suck in oxygen, but I could not. I was suffocating, and yet, I did not die. My flesh was burning, and yet, I did not die. My brain was being ripped apart from the pain and sensations in my body, and yet, I did not die. The flames of hell were burning my eyes, my tongue, my hands, and my belly from the crown of my head to the soles of my feet, I was in excruciating pain. The burning, boiling, searing, brimstone and sulfur of hell were penetrating every fiber of my being, and yet, I did not die. I am not in the least exaggerating my experience, if anything I am under-rating it.

As I was going through these terrible sensations, I felt an upward thrust pushing me toward the top of the lake of fire. A strong type of current was dragging me along. And then I came to the surface. I began bobbing up and down as I was being moved along, turning, end over end, head over heels, rolling and tumbling with the swirling masses of those around me in the violent waves and currents of hell. By now, you would think that all of my feelings would have been gone, burned out into nonexistence, that all of my five senses would have been seared into nothingness. You would think that I would have gone into absolute and total shock, that I would have been virtually and completely numb. But that was not the case. Every one of my five senses was still very much alive.

I could touch, taste, hear, smell; I could see the torments of hell. Now I can tell you, my friend, by personal experience that the most extreme and bizarre torments that a person could ever experience on Earth is nothing compared to the never-ending torments of hell.

Worms in Hell

In hell there is a worm. It is the worm of your memory, the anguish of your soul, the worm of your conscience. It is the thought of lost happiness and lost opportunities to get right with God. The worm is the reality of the fact that you heard this message—you heard this truth—but you did not believe it. You read the Bible, but you did not live it. You could have walked with God, but you did not. And now your memory will eat away at you forever. Your memory will devour you from the inside out and yet never cease to exist. Oh, how terrible! In hell there are untold billions of husbands and wives, fathers and mothers, sons and daughters, hopelessly lost forever swallowed up in the fires of hell, gnawed by the worm that never dies.

The Scriptures also imply that in hell there is another kind of worm. In my fictitious book called the Chronicles of Micah, I reveal an experience that Micah had in hell with worms. As Micah was pulled along in the lake of fire, he noticed that there were some other creatures in this boiling molasses of pain. They looked like some kind of large, extremely ugly, terrifying worms.

They would come to the surface then disappear, then return to the surface and disappear again. It was as if they were searching and hungering for something. Or was it somebody? It sent chills up and down his spine, even though he was in excruciating pain. Unconsciously he found himself trying to hide from them. But he could not run or hide. About twenty feet away from him, a number of these large ugly worms broke the surface then disappeared, broke the surface then disappeared, and broke the surface again. Then he noticed that they were coming straight toward him.

In less than ten seconds, they were upon him. Not only were they upon him, but they were digging their way into him. They pushed their way into his already hurting, burning flesh. They squirmed and pushed and wiggled their way into his body. He could feel them crawling inside of him. Absolute disgust and dismay filled his heart and mind as they explored every fiber of his being. They even pushed their way up his throat and into his brain. They would either squirm out of his ears, or they would push their way past his eyes, coming out of the sockets, only to enter back into him somewhere else. He couldn't get them out, and he couldn't stop them. They were driving him insane.

"Thy pomp is brought down to the grave, and the noise of thy viols: the worm is spread under thee, and the worms cover thee" (Isa. 14:1).

"And they shall go forth, and look upon the carcases of the men that have transgressed against me: for their worm shall not die, neither shall their fire be quenched; and they shall be an abhorring unto all flesh" (Isa. 66:24).

Jesus made the same statement about the worm in *Mark 9:44, 46 and 48;"Where their worm dieth not, and the fire is not quenched."*

ETERNITY IN HELL

There seemed to be no end to this nightmare called hell. A second dragged into an hour. A minute turned into a year, and an hour became an everlasting eternity. This was just the beginning of forever. There is no end to this place called hell. There is no escape. There is no exit. There is no way out. Hell is eternal; it is forever. Some would have you believe otherwise. You and I both know without a shadow of a doubt that God is eternal.

"For I am the LORD, I change not" (Mal. 3:6a).

"Jesus Christ the same yesterday, and today, and forever" (Heb. 13:8).

His Word is eternal; heaven and earth shall pass away. If God is everlasting, His Word is everlasting, and heaven is everlasting. Then so is the wrath, the anger, and the judgment of God everlasting.

"And the smoke of their torment ascendeth up for ever and ever: and they have no rest day or night" (Rev. 14:11).

Some believe that when Christ died upon the cross that the sacrifice that Jesus made changed the Father. But that is an utter and horrendous lie. What Christ did on the cross was never meant to change God the Father. For God does not need to be changed.

"Every good gift and every perfect gift is from above, and cometh down from the Father of lights, with whom is no variableness, neither shadow of turning" (James 1:17).

But Jesus' death on the cross was meant to change you and me. Have you ever stopped to think who spoke hell into existence? Who created hell? The Scriptures clearly declare that everything that was created was created by Jesus Christ. You heard correctly, the Scriptures clearly declare that God the Father created all things by the hands of Jesus.

"All things were made by him; and without him was not any thing made that was made" (John 1:3).

"For by him were all things created, that are in heaven, and that are in earth, visible and invisible, whether they be thrones, or dominions, or

principalities, or powers: all things were created by him, and for him: And he is before all things, and by him all things consist"(Col 1:16-17).

Our blessed Savior and Redeemer, He who shed His precious blood for our redemption, gave His life and gave His all for humanity, brought hell into existence. Therefore hell must need to exist for the safety and good of all creation. Hell was not created for man but for the devil and his angels. Jesus longs to rescue the human race from this terrible and horrible place.

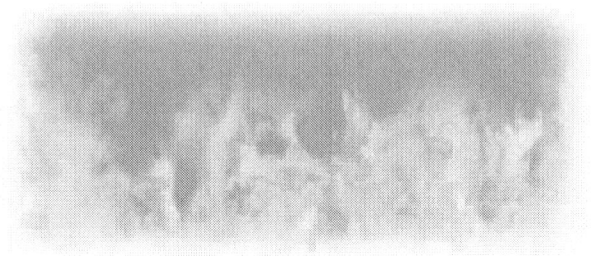

CHAPTER FIVE

NO LOVE IN HELL

If you can imagine in the midst of the pain and agony, another even much greater and terrifying torment began to flood my soul. It was emotional, spiritual, psychological, and mental. Here in this place, this bubbling, boiling slime pit called hell, there is absolutely no love. It is totally void of all love. Even when I was a sinner, I was surrounded by the love of God, His goodness, provision, and blessings. I may not have recognized or even realized it. Whether I knew it or not, God was watching over me. He was protecting, helping, and reaching out to me, even though I was not serving Him or loving Him. A guardian angel was there all the time, though I could not see him. Jesus said:

"Take heed that ye despise not one of these little ones; for I say unto you, That in heaven their angels do always behold the face of my Father which is in heaven" (Matt. 18:10).

Nature, birds, animals, and all of creation display the unfathomable love of God. The shining sun, the green grass, the budding flowers, the blue gray waters of the sea, the light blue skies, the glowing moon, and the sparkling stars at night. They all declare God's awesome love for His creation. The beautiful fragrances that float upon the wind and the singing birds with their beautiful songs declare His love. God has blessed us and revealed Himself to us by His awesome creation according to Scriptures on God's goodness.

"Or despisest thou the riches of his goodness and forbearance and longsuffering; not knowing that the goodness of God leadeth thee to repentance?" (Rom. 2:4).

"That ye may be the children of your Father which is in heaven: for he maketh his sun to rise on the evil and on the good, and sendeth rain on the just and on the unjust" (Matt. 5:45).

We need to understand that unconverted, unregenerate man has accepted and believed the lies of evolution. But it is a lie from the satanic realm.

"In whom the god of this world hath blinded the minds of them which believe not, lest the light of the glorious gospel of Christ, who is the image of God, should shine unto them"(2 Cor. 4:4).

For God is the Author, Creator, Maker, Architect and Master Designer of all of creation. God gave us the breath we are breathing, the clothes we are wearing, the food we are eating, the body we are living in; it all comes from God. He gave us all of the talents and abilities we have in order to put

31

within our hands these possessions. All that we have that is good and beautiful, lovely and beneficial, comes from God. It is God's divine marriage proposal, a divine romance. For you see, God is calling, pleading, imploring, and asking us to follow Him into light everlasting.

"Behold, I stand at the door, and knock: if any man hear my voice, and open the door, I will come in to him, and will sup with him, and he with me" (Rev. 3:20).

"We love him, because he first loved us." (1 John 4:19).

Jesus paid the ultimate price for the hand of His bride. He bought us with every drop of His precious blood in His body. And He longs for us to follow Him down the wedding aisle to the throne of His Father, to be one with Him forever. You see, my friend, God is striving to lead us to a place of turning our backs upon our selfish lives, to crucify and mortify the corruptible and damnable seed of selfishness, which is the very nature of the devil and his fallen angels—the demonic horde. We must believe on the Lord Jesus Christ. We must walk in His divine nature of love so that we can be one with Him forever.

"Every good gift and perfect gift is from above, and cometh down from the Father of lights, with whom is no variableness, neither shadow of turning" (James 1:17).

Are you taking carelessly God's abundant goodness, His kindness, His patience, and the fact that He has suffered a long time waiting for you?

Do you not grasp that His kindness is meant to cause you to turn away from selfishness?

Our number one desire should be to love Him with all of our hearts. True Christianity is simply striving to love God with all of your heart, spirit, soul, mind, and body. We love Him because He first loved us. Love our neighbors as we love ourselves. We need to respond to His amazing love.

All of creation will be our jury, and they will declare us guilty of the most perverse wickedness and corruption if we do not. To think that we would turn down such a wonderful and awesome gift from God is unfathomable. The reality is that Jesus is offering us to be made one with Himself simply by acknowledging our wickedness and by forsaking all in order to follow him. Yielding to the divine grace of His nature within us. While we have an opportunity, we need to respond to His unspeakable and amazing love.

But in that God-forsaken, burning slime pit called hell there is no love whatsoever. The goodness of God, the long-sufferings of God, the kindness of God, the blessings of God, and the mercies of God are all gone, eternally lost because people refused to listen. Masses have refused to obey. Multitudes have refused to love Him, even though He invited them to be His bride, His beloved companion for eternity.

All Alone in Hell

A loneliness and emptiness beyond description descended upon me. Even though I bumped into many others, there was no communication. You have no recognition of friends and relatives. Those in hell are tormented devils and souls. They are filled with dreadful shrieks, screams caused by the fierceness of their pains. There are fearful blasphemies against God's power and justice who keeps them there. The torments of fellow sufferers do nothing to relieve you of your miseries. It only increases them. And every soul that you lead into hell with you will only magnify your sorrows a hundredfold. Dad and mom, pastor and preacher, teacher and politician, Can you live with yourself knowing your taking some you love to hell with you?

There are many who think that hell will be party time. They laugh, they mock, and they scoff at the reality of hell. They laugh at them who tell them of a place called hell. Their destruction is their own fault, and they will never forget it. And in life they refused to be one with God in order to continue to be one with the world. In hell they are all alone forever. Just this thought should cause us to turn from our selfish ways.

"But be ye doers of the word, and not hearers only, deceiving your own selves" (James 1:22).

Please, listen to me. This book could be an answer to someone's prayers for you, someone who knows you and is pleading for your soul. And if you reject this message, throughout eternity you will be screaming and crying, begging and pleading for water and all of your other desires. The rich man cried out for water, but it was too late. And you will be tormented forever with both natural and sinful, unfulfilled desires. Your natural and spiritual selfish thirst will never be fulfilled, never satisfied. Your thirsts will never be quenched, and the agony of it will never end.

Endless Pain in Hell

In hell there is no relief, no freedom from pain. One's body does not go numb; rather, the pain intensifies. Every part of the soul, body, mind, emotions, and our total being is tormented at once. The human body is a wonderful and marvelous creation.

"I will praise thee; for I am fearfully and wonderfully made: marvelous are thy works; and that my soul knoweth right well" (Ps. 139:14).

And yet, amazingly the soul of man also has a body. The natural eye cannot see the body of the soul, but that does not mean it does not exist. Your soul in this life looks exactly like your physical body. But in heaven, if you die in Christ, you will receive a glorified body, a body that is glorious and amazing. There'll be no natural blood that flows through your new body. But the very Spirit of God Himself flows through your veins. We will never need sleep. This new body can endure any kind of harshness or atmosphere or environment. It will be absolutely indestructible, eternal, and immortal. According to the Scriptures the unrepentant sinner Himself shall also receive a new body. This body will be cast into the lake of fire with the devil and his angels *(see John 5:28-29, 1 Thes. 4:16, and Dan. 12:2).*

God must put an end to the sinful shenanigans of the satanic nature. The pain, suffering, agony, and torment of eternal damnation restrain and hinder the satanic nature. But it cannot cleanse the human heart, soul, mind, will, and emotions from the seed of sin. Only through the sacrificial work of Jesus Christ and loving Him can our hearts be cleansed from this dreadful seed of sin.

How long I had been in hell, I do not know. It seemed like an eternity. I had been crying out in pain and agony unconsciously, screaming and wailing like the rest of the damned. And yet my cries were of a totally different nature. Their cries were cursing, profanity, wickedness, begging, and promises of repentance if given another chance. Curses were only to be followed by more curses.

The realm of hell is filled with the noise of the damned, weeping and wailing and crying. They were shouting and screaming and yelling and moaning in terrible overwhelming pain. And yet those who are in hell now understand their spiritual condition and that their punishment is just and proper. They understand that they alone are to blame for their present situation and eternal damnation.

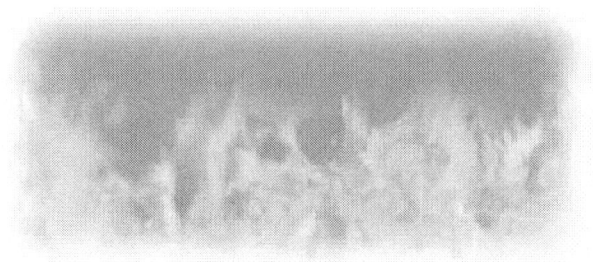

CHAPTER SIX

Cry for Help in Hell

Now my cries were to God, justifying, praising, worshiping, and acknowledging that from God came my help. I remember screaming in pain that God is righteous in His judgments and that He is true and faithful and worthy of all glory and honor. From my heart and soul, out of my mouth came a nonstop flow of love and devotion, praise and worship to the Three in One.

It might be hard to believe that someone filled with such overwhelming pain and agony could be worshiping and praising the One who was causing such horrible afflictions, and yet that's what I was doing. The Scriptures declare for out of the abundance of the heart the mouth speaks. Then from somewhere within I cried out for deliverance.

"Though he slay me, yet will I trust in him: but I will maintain mine own ways before him" (Job 13:15).

"A good man out of the good treasure of his heart bringeth forth that which is good; and an evil man out of the evil treasure of his heart bringeth forth that which is evil: for of the abundance of the heart his mouth speaketh. And why call ye me, Lord, Lord, and do not the things which I say?" (Luke 6:45-46).

God Heard Me in Hell

In the midst of my prayers, I heard a voice that seemed to come from heaven. It was A majestic thunderous and awesome sound. This voice completely overwhelmed all of the sensations I was experiencing at that moment. It literally grabbed hold of me and placed me in a protective bubble. All of my blistered and burning flesh was instantly healed and made whole. My hair, clothes, and body were returned to their original condition just as they were before my journey began. The love and goodness of God came rushing back in to my heart and mind.

The sorrows and woes of hell disappeared. This voice had an amazing effect upon hell. It shook the very foundations of the lake of fire itself. I heard the audible voice of God say, " Let My servant go." The bowels of hell twisted and turned as if in torment. They ripped apart like the Red Sea must have when Moses stretched forth his rod. Hell had no choice but to obey the voice of the Lord of heaven, earth, and hell.

"And said, I cried by reason of my affliction unto the LORD, and he heard me; out of the belly of hell cried I, and thou heardest my voice" (Jonah 2:2).

"The sorrows of hell compassed me about; the snares of death prevented me; In my distress I called upon the LORD, and cried to my God: and he did hear my voice out of his temple, and my cry did enter into his ears. Then the earth shook and trembled; the foundations of heaven moved and shook, because he was wroth. There went up a smoke out of his nostrils, and fire out of his mouth devoured: coals were kindled by it. He bowed the heavens also, and came down; and darkness was under his feet" (2 Sam. 22:6-10).

Out of Hell

At that very moment, it was almost like hell itself vomited me out. Incredibly it felt like I was being shot out of a canon. The next thing I knew, I was standing on the edge of a high and steep cliff. No longer was I in hell, but I was standing on the lip of a cliff looking straight down into the ocean of torment I had just been suffering in. The ocean of hell was still bubbling, boiling, and churning. And I could feel some of the heat of it hitting my body. The stench of it was still suffocating.

I would say that the cliff was probably over a thousand feet high. As a looked around, I noticed that the land around me was virtually flat, with no vegetation. It all looked like it was compacted brownish, gray soil, with rocks and boulders. As I looked behind me there seemed to be a mountain range on the far horizon. As I looked to my right side, I noticed that in the distance there was what looked to be a wide, dark, slow-flowing river. It was pouring its contents like Niagara Falls over the edge of the cliff into the yawning mouth of hell.

But there was something very strange and eerie about this river. I did not want anything to do with this river. Actually there was this overwhelming desire in my heart to run as far away from it as I could. I knew that there was something very wrong about what I was seeing. In my heart I sensed that whatever the river was, it would bring to me tremendous pain and sorrow perhaps even more so than what I had experienced in the bottomless pit of hell. And yet, with this knowledge, this foreboding and dread in my heart, I knew that I must go to this river.

The Spirit of God was prompting me to go and investigate. So instead of running away from this river, I found myself walking along the edge of the cliff, toward the river. As I got closer and closer, I began to tremble and shake. I could barely breathe. I had to take short gasps of breath. I could not believe, and I did not want to believe what I was seeing before my very eyes.

Broad and Wide Road

This broad and wide, Dark River was not flowing with water, as I had supposed. It was made up of multitudes and multitudes of people. Masses of humanity without number.

"Enter ye in at the strait gate: for wide is the gate, and broad is the way, that leadeth to destruction, and many there be which go in thereat" (Matt. 7:13).

I could see that there were those of all nations, tongues and peoples. I saw the dress of every religious group you could imagine. Upon this road there was a range of people who were both young and elderly. And by looking at their mannerisms and dress, you could determine to some extent what their livelihoods were. There were people of all professions—doctors, nurses, plumbers, professors, pastors, teachers, housewives, factory workers, policemen, farmers, milk men, bankers, military personnel, politicians, and world rulers.

"And he saith unto me, The waters which thou sawest, where the whore sitteth, are peoples, and multitudes, and nations, and tongues" (Rev. 17:15).

"Multitudes, multitudes in the valley of decision: for the day of the LORD is near in the valley of decision" (Joel 3:14).

As I drew nearer and nearer to this river, I could see that the people were walking on what looked to be a very wide asphalt road that made its winding way as far as my eyes could see into the horizon. Every inch of the road was packed to capacity with humanity, like sardines in a can. It seemed almost impossible for people to be packed so tight and so close together.

Now this road came right to the very edge of the cliff. At the cliff it broke off with jagged edges hanging over emptiness. It looked like a road would if an earthquake had transpired with the earth dropping out from underneath a major highway! And below this broken highway was the yawning, never-satisfied mouth of hell.

CHAPTER SEVEN

Headed to Destruction

As I came closer to this river of humanity I found myself unconsciously looking deep into the faces of those who were walking on this broad and wide road. None of them, I literally mean that none of them seemed to be in the least bit concerned at all about where they were headed. They did not seem to be concerned about their future or where they were going.

They did not seem to question the direction in which they were walking. Many were laughing and jesting. Others simply engrossed in conversation. Others caught up in their own problems. As I looked upon their faces I could perceive in my heart who they were and what they were going through.

I knew in my heart that by the Spirit of God I was experiencing their sorrows, pains, loneliness, and depression. I also perceived the hopes, dreams, and visions that they had in their hearts, that which they had not yet apprehended or achieved. But not one of them seemed to be concerned about what was about to happen. Or where they were going. It was as if they were sleepwalking, like they were slumbering not realizing the danger that was just before them. It was as if they were blind to their eternal damnation.

"And the cares of this world, and the deceitfulness of riches, and the lusts of other things entering in, choke the word, and it becometh unfruitful" *(Mark 4:19).*

"And he spake a parable unto them, saying, The ground of a certain rich man brought forth plentifully: And he thought within himself, saying, What shall I do, because I have no room where to bestow my fruits? And he said, This will I do: I will pull down my barns, and build greater; and there will I bestow all my fruits and my goods. And I will say to my soul, Soul, thou hast much goods laid up for many years; take thine ease, eat, drink, and be merry. But God said unto him, Thou fool, this night thy soul shall be required of thee: then whose shall those things be, which thou hast provided? So is he that layeth up treasure for himself, and is not rich toward God" (Luke 12:16-21).

At about twenty feet from the end of the road a small handful of them would seem to begin to wake up. At that moment it would become a totally different story. The reality of the situation seemed to finally dawn upon their faces. As they were pushed forward they began to try to push back against the oncoming masses. And the more they were pushed forward, the more frantic they became. They began to scream and cry and yell for help. But it was too late; they could not detach themselves from the masses. They were pushed forward, inch by inch, foot by foot. Those on the very edge of the cliff would seem to lose their mind in absolute terror as they saw more clearly what was awaiting them at the bottom of the cliff. It was as if their eyes were popping out of their head.

Never have I seen faces so contorted with absolute horror and fear. I knew they could not believe what they were seeing. They began to push back with all of their might, clawing, hitting, scratching, trying to crawl over the top of those who were unwillingly pushing them to their destruction and damnation.

Screams of unbelievable horror came from their lips as they would try to hang on. Shouting and screaming with such deep desperation that it breaks my heart retelling it to you. It did not seem as if those who were only a few feet back could hear or see what was taking place until it was their turn. Or maybe they simply chose to ignore the commotion, because it did not yet involve them. They were so caught up in their daily living until destruction came upon them without warning.

"For when they shall say, Peace and safety; then sudden destruction cometh upon them, as travail upon a woman with child; and they shall not escape" (1 Thess. 5:3).

Into the Abyss of Hell

As the people on the broad and wide asphalt road fell over the jagged edge, I watched them dig their fingernails into its unyielding surface. Not being able to hold on, they would continue to claw at the rough cliff walls. Leaving trails of their precious human blood.

The cliff wall was covered and matted with human blood, flesh, and bones. You could hear their pitiful screams for help as they tried to stop their descent into hell. As they plunged toward hell I would watch them spinning and tumbling head over heels. No horror flick ever made could express the absolute terror and horror I was watching take place before my eyes. These peoples' worst nightmares were coming to pass— nightmares that would last throughout eternity.

When their bodies hit the burning, liquefied lava of hell it would create a splash like that of a rock dropping into a puddle of mud. For a few seconds I could see them struggling, still floating on the surface of the lake of lava, like a leaf on the water. Their clothes would catch on fire. Their hair would go up in flames and be consumed. Their identities were lost. No longer could you tell that they were male or female.

Their nationalities, their ages, even the color of their skin was devoured in the burning torments of hell. Oh you cannot believe the terrible, heart-wrenching screams as they hit the surface and began to burn. They would slowly sink into the burning mud of hell, swallowed up in the never-ending undercurrents of this ocean of damnation. These were men and women, young and old, grandmas and grandpas, and teenagers. These were people of all nations and cultures from every diverse aspect of life. For hell is not a respecter of people.

Hell is Enlarging Itself

If this in itself is not horrible enough, then even more heart wrenching is the fact that this river of humanity is seemingly never-ending. Neither does it slow up. It just keeps flowing unrelentingly, as far as the eye could see. At the time if I had a pair of binoculars, I still would not have been able to see the end to this road. I have read somewhere that there is an estimated 6.6 billion people on the Earth right now.

Out of that number, over 235,000 people are dying every day. If it takes you five hours to read this book, by the time you finish reading, over 48,955 people will have died and gone to their eternal destiny. That means 9,791 people die every hour, and 163 people die every minute. Out of 6.6 billion people only 350 million confess to be Protestant Christians. How many of them truly love God and have forsaken the world? Only God truly knows.

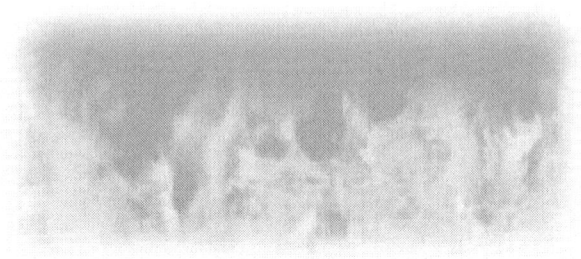

CHAPTER EIGHT

God's Heart Broken

As I watched these masses of humanity falling into the bottomless pit of hell I literally could not handle it. I ran from the edge of the cliff alongside this road of damned humanity like one who has lost his mind. I wanted to escape the sight of the pain and agony etched in peoples' faces as they were falling over the cliff. My heart felt like it was totally and mortally wounded.

I felt like I was being stabbed with a huge knife that was slowly twisting and turning inside of me in my heart. My heart felt like it was being torn out of my chest. Now, if I felt this way, can you imagine how God feels?

People believe that after Jesus suffered on the cross that He no longer suffers. But this is a sadly mistaken assumption. For the Father, Son, and the Holy Ghost are still in deep agony and pain over the fate of humanity. God's heart is broken over the

loss of humanity and of the angelic realm that
disobeyed and rebelled against Him.

I Have to Do Something

I ran from the dreadful scene before my
eyes. I ran until I could run no more. Out of breath I
finally slowed to a walk. As I continued to walk, I
realized that I must do something about these
masses and masses of people that were headed
straight to hell.

I was still walking alongside this wide,
broad, river of humanity but away from the cliff. So
I began to shout to them, pleading and begging
them to come off the road. I warned the people with
all the compassion of my heart, with tears cascading
down my face, flowing like a river, weeping, and
pleading nonstop.

*"Oh that my head were waters, and mine eyes a
fountain of tears, that I might weep day and night
for the slain of the daughter of my people!" (Jer.
9:1).*

*"Rivers of waters run down mine eyes, because
they keep not thy law" (Ps. 119:136).*

I tried everything I could, knowing that
every minute that passed more and more people
were falling over the cliff. And because I had
experienced the pains and torments of hell I knew
what they were about to experience and that they
would never get out. I was preaching the thunder

and the lightning of heaven. Then I would speak the love and mercy of the goodness of God. I preached the reality of Jesus and His atoning sacrificial work. With all the truths that I had available I declared God's kingdom that I might rescue some.

They Would Not Listen

Many of these people on the road would stare at me as if I had lost my mind. Some would yell back at me, telling me to mind my own business. Some yelled that they were Christians, and that they were going to heaven. And others would seem to listen, with tears flowing down their cheeks. They would say that they wanted to come off of the broad and wide way, but they could not, that their hearts were too addicted to sin.

They did not believe that Jesus had the power to deliver them, that they were beyond hope. Some said that they had blasphemed the Holy Ghost and therefore there was no salvation available for them. Others declared that they loved sin too much to let go of it. The demonic hordes were whispering in their ears, lying to them that God would not forgive them, that they were too far gone, or that hell was just a make-believe imaginary place.

"But if our gospel be hid, it is hid to them that are lost: In whom the god of this world hath blinded the minds of them which believe not, lest the light of the glorious gospel of Christ, who is the image of God, should shine unto them" (2 Cor. 4:3-4).

Laborers Few

I knew in my heart that the work before me was too great for one person alone. I desperately needed help to reach these this multitude of lost souls. One person by himself could not make barely a dent in evangelizing this ocean of humanity. I began searching to find someone, anyone, who could help me reach all these people.

Clusters of Saints

As I looked out across the flat plateaus, I could see clusters of objects in the distance. I could not make out what they were, but they seemed to be shining with a brilliant white. They were not on the broad and wide road but directly off to the side of it. As I moved farther up the road I saw that these white objects were in what appeared to be small and large groupings.

And as I looked out over the plain, I noticed there were more of these clusters. Not just one or two but hundreds of them were scattered across the horizon. Some appeared to be extremely large, others were very small with many different sizes in between. As I drew closer to the first one, I discerned there was some type of movement taking place in these brilliant white clusters. As I drew closer it became apparent to me what they were.

These clusters were made up of people wearing glistening white robes. They were all grouped together in circles, facing inward, sometimes back to back. Their backs were to the river of humanity walking on the broad and wide road and to all else. The closer I came near these clusters, the more it became clear what was happening.

Many of those within these clusters had their hands lifted up toward heaven. As I got closer I could see smiles of joy radiating from their faces. Tears were running down their cheeks. They were singing amazing and beautiful songs of love for Christ. At times one or more would break out in what seemed to be a prophetic Word.

From what I could hear, most of these songs were about how much God loved them and about the blessings that would overtake them in their walk with the Lord. These songs said that they were precious and important to Jesus and to the heavenly Father. I realized automatically who these people in white must be. They were fellow believers and saints in Christ—brothers and sisters in Jesus Christ. All of these clusters of saints seemed to be lost in their devotion to and for God.

But they seemed to be lost, totally and completely oblivious to the masses of humanity that were just a few feet away from them being led to an everlasting, never-ending, eternal damnation. They were enraptured in their own little spiritual experiences. They were enthralled with singing songs of praise and worship. There was no denying the sincerity; it was evident in their involvement and enthusiasm. But what good is sincerity, blessings, joyful spiritual experiences, and Holy Ghost parties if you are not concerned about anyone else except your own little group. It's what Scripture refers to as sounding brass and twinkling cymbals.

"Though I speak with the tongues of men and of angels, and have not charity, I am become as sounding brass, or a tinkling cymbal. And though I have the gift of prophecy, and understand all mysteries, and all knowledge; and though I have all faith, so that I could remove mountains, and have not charity, I am nothing. And though I bestow all my goods to feed the poor, and though I give my body to be burned, and have not charity, it profiteth me nothing" (1 Cor. 13:1-3).

A divine and supernatural urgency rose up in my heart. I tried to push my way into one of these clusters. And as I did I found myself yelling and pointing to the river of humanity. It was not anger, self-righteousness, or disgust that moved me but God's love. It was His overwhelming love and compassion that was being shed abroad in my heart by the Holy Ghost. It was love for the unconverted, lost, and blind sinners.

I desperately needed help to reach the lost masses upon the road of destruction. I knew in my heart that the heart of God was being broken because His people were not having compassion upon those who had not yet come to love and know Him, those who had not yet been converted and become new creatures in Christ Jesus.

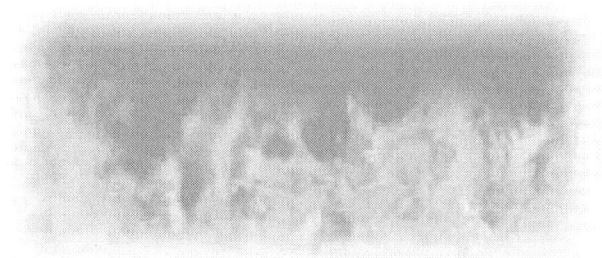

CHAPTER NINE

This is Not Our Cross

When I was finally able to get one group's attention, they looked at me as one who looks upon a lunatic. "Look. Look," I said, pointing toward the broad and wide road. "Millions upon millions of men and women, young and old, are only a short distance from your cluster. And they are headed right for hell. We have got to do something. Please, please help me to reach them!"

The worship and praise stopped. No one in the group moved. It was like they were in a stupor. Since it seemed like I had their attention, I continued with my exhortation for them to help me reach the lost. Finally, one of the men spoke up. "Excuse me, brother, but God has not given us a spirit of condemnation. It seems to us that you are trying to bring us into bondage with this legalism. Whom the Son has set free is free indeed.

You're putting this heavy guilt trip on us, and that definitely cannot be God. And to be quite blunt with you evangelism is not our ministry." For a moment I was totally dumbfounded. Surely this brother in Christ had to be joking. There is no way that anybody could be that ignorant of God's Word and God's heart. For a minute I was in such shock that I could not answer them. The Holy Spirit rose up within me, and out of my mouth came Scripture after Scripture.

"And Jesus said unto them, Come ye after me, and I will make you to become fishers of men" (Mark 1:17).

"For the Son of man is come to seek and to save that which was lost" (Luke 19:10).

I kept pleading and imploring them to help me pull humanity from the flames of hell. But no matter what I said, they did not seem to understand what I was saying. I could not get them to move. I remember standing there completely frustrated, weeping, and crying uncontrollably. Not only for the damned but for those who called themselves believers.

Somehow the enemy of our souls has deceived the majority of the church into a place of spiritual complacency and pacifism. Now, there is no denying that there is some small measure of concern for the lost. But there's not the red-hot fervency and overwhelming love for souls that we should have. It is so sad that it seems that those within the body of Christ do not believe in hell themselves. God's number one concern is for souls to be saved.

"And he said to them all, If any man will come after me, let him deny himself, and take up his cross daily, and follow me" (Luke 9:23).

In the Harvest Field

I fell to my knees on the ground under tremendous sorrow and the heavy burden that was upon my heart, surrounded by these brothers and sisters in Christ. I closed my eyes as I wept with heavy sobs praying that God would open the eyes of humanity and of His church. I prayed that God would forgive me for my lack of concern and love. I prayed that the Lord of the harvest would raise up laborers for the harvest field. How long I prayed, I do not know. When I finally opened up my eyes, I found myself back in my barracks upon my knees in prayer.

Willie Wine was on his knees right off to the side of me. I saw a strange expression on his face. Neither one of us said anything for a while. I noticed there was no music or sound of the men in the background. I asked him what was going on. He told me that they heard me screaming, crying, and wailing in the most unbelievable, heartrending and horrifying ways. He said they were all scared and ran for it. Willie asked me what had happened. During all the hours that I was experiencing this supernatural visitation from the Lord, Willie had been in prayer right at my side. I tried to describe to him everything that happened. Partly due to this visitation, a miniature revival hit our military base.

From that moment forth an overwhelming burden came upon me. My love for Christ and souls went way beyond what I had experienced before. I became extremely desperate to reach souls for Christ. On the streets and highways, malls and shopping centers, Laundromats, and bar rooms. Wherever I could reach people, I was there.

Compassion for the Lost

After this particular experience, an overpowering love began to possess me! My heart was filled with immense concern for the lost and unsaved. I looked for men up and down the hallways and in the tunnels of our military facility.

One time when I witnessed to a man about the reality of heaven and hell, he basically said he did not want to hear it. God's love was so strong within me I instantly dropped to my knees and wrapped my arms around his legs. I begged him to give his heart to Jesus. I did not want to see him lose his soul and spend eternity in hell.

Arrested for Preaching

The compassion of God was flowing in me like a mighty river. It was so strong that an overwhelming desire came upon me to reach as many people as I could at one time. The idea came to me that I could reach more men on that military base if I went to the movie theater we had on the island.

I remember going to the very front row of this movie theater. I sat down shaking and waiting, wondering if what I was about to do was right. I looked at my watch and knew the movie would begin any minute. Just before they started the movie, I stood up on the ledge where the movie screen was attached to the floor.

I stood there shaking for a while, trying to get up enough nerve to open my mouth. The men in the theater began to yell for me to get off the stage and sit down. Instead, I opened my mouth and began to preach. As I preached, I could see the Holy Spirit was beginning to move upon the hearts of the audience.

It wasn't long before the military police showed up to arrest me. It was amazing that they did not take me by force, but instead waited for me to finish. When I finished what the Lord had told me to say, the police told me to come off the stage. The two of them grabbed my arms and dragged me out of the theater.

They arrested me, put me in their military vehicle, and took me to jail. They asked what I was trying to do in the theater. I took the opportunity to share with them how Jesus had radically changed my life by saving my soul. I told them Jesus wanted to do the same for them. They released me without pressing charges.

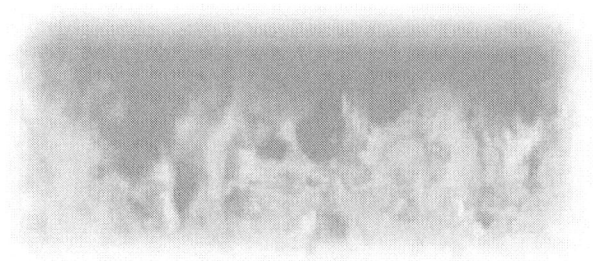

CHAPTER TEN

Why This Book?

First, let me say that I never intended to write about this encounter with God. To me, it was extremely personal and overwhelming. When I approached a well-known publishing company to publish a book for me, it was actually for another book. But as I began to share some of my testimony with the lady who is in charge of the acquisitions, she strongly suggested that I should write a book about this experience.

Truthfully, I was very reluctant at the beginning. But as she continued to encourage me, I began to see that this was a part of God's plan possibly to stir the hearts of God's people to begin to evangelize in a greater way. Off the top of my head I can quickly count seven benefits to sharing with you my experiences:

1.To create a deeper love and passion for souls!

2.To wake up a sleeping church!

3.For the salvation of sinners.

4.To instigate divine visitations in the lives of fellow believers.

5.That the fear of the Lord might come back into the earth and in into His church.

6.So we might be ready for the final outpouring of the early and latter rain.

7.That revival would break forth in the salvation of souls throughout the body of Christ.

What Will You Do?

Brothers and sisters, now that you have been confronted with the reality of masses of people headed to hell, what are you going to do about it? Will we become coworkers together with Christ?

"But let every man prove his own work, and then shall he have rejoicing in himself alone, and not in another. For every man shall bear his own burden" (Gal. 6:4-5).

How can we allow humanity, our moms and dads, brothers and sisters, aunts and uncles, sons and daughters, neighbors and friends go to hell without warning them? Without telling them the truth? May God stir up our hearts that we may go forth and proclaim the glorious Good News that Jesus Christ took our place so that we would not have to suffer the penalty of eternal damnation!

It is the will of God for every one of us within the body of Christ to have a burden for souls and to evangelize. It is our responsibility to share the Good News of Jesus Christ.

Note to Sinners and Backsliders

For those who possibly are not right with God, the story I have just shared with you truly happened to me. The Bible says that:

"By faith Noah, being warned of God of things not seen as yet, moved with fear, prepared an ark to the saving of his house; by the which he condemned the world, and became heir of the righteousness which is by faith" (Heb. 11:7).

God is moving in my heart with tremendous love and fear for you and for all of those who might not love God. I beg you and plead with you, in the name of Jesus Christ of Nazareth, to turn from your selfish, sinful, wicked ways and claim a new life in Jesus Christ. Or you will go to a burning hell. Once you have crossed the dark river of death, never more will you see a flower or green pastures or rolling oceans. Never will you again enjoy a glass of clear pure water or the simple pleasures of life. You will never again enjoy the sweet communion with those you love and know. But you will be lost forever in the endless ages of eternal darkness and fire.

Darkness and pain, torment and sorrow will be your eternal destiny. Shaking hands with a preacher will not save you. Putting your name on a church membership list will not do it. Giving money to a ministry or doing good deeds of any kind will not get you to heaven. We must repent of willful, known sin, and we must have a Godly sorrow for our actions.

We must ask God, out of the depths of our hearts, to forgive us. And no matter how great our sin is, if we are sincere and no longer want to stay in our sins, God will deliver and forgive and accept us. Oh, sinner, be warned while there is yet time, and the eyes of the Savior still plead, and Jesus still beckons. Leave the broad and wide path of a selfish life, which leads to hell. And walk upon the straight and narrow way, which leads to heaven.

Remember how the demons cried out and asked Jesus whether He had come to torment them before their time? Are we so foolish as to not be moved by the realities of hell or to make light of them? Christianity consists of a new heart and a new life, dedicated and committed to not sinning. It is living for the glory of God. If your heart and life has not been changed by God, if you are still living in open rebellion and known disobedience to the Word and will of God, and you are not concerned about it, you have no right to assume you are going to heaven.

The devil and his demons will have the right to grab you by the hair, by your arms and legs, and pull you to hell with them. Sin is worse than hell because sin made it necessary for Jesus to create such a place called hell. It is the ultimate conclusion of a sinful life. Please, flee from sin! Flee from living for yourself. Flee from being self-pleasing, self-serving, self-loving, and self-centered. When you die, it will be too late to turn away from your sins.

All opportunity to turn to God ends at death. Unless you turn from your selfishness and run to Jesus Christ and believe on Him who is our only hope, you will curse God eternally. And you will never die to the pains, agonies, terrors, horrors, and sorrows of hell. You will never experience the glory of heaven.

"Many will say to me in that day, Lord, Lord, have we not prophesied in thy name? and in thy name have cast out devils? and in thy name done many wonderful works? and then will I profess unto them, I never knew you: depart from me, ye that work iniquity" (Matt. 7:22).

I pray with all of my heart that this experience God allowed me to have in order to warn you will cause you to look to the loving Savior who poured out His lifeblood for you and who was nailed to the cross for your sins. He lovingly and longingly desires you to become one of His children.

Won't you believe upon Him today? Call out to Him today. He will in no way cast out any who come to Him. Please, please turn from your wicked, evil, and self- centered ways. Love Him who first loved us. Let God give you a new heart and nature, a heart that loves, serves, and follows God. I hope to see you in heaven!

ABOUT THE AUTHOR

Dr. Michael and Kathleen Yeager have served as pastors/apostles, missionaries, evangelists, broadcasters and authors for overt four decades. They flow in the gifts of the Holy Spirit, teaching the Word of God with wonderful signs and miracles following in confirmation of God's Word. In 1983, they began Jesus is Lord Ministries International, Biglerville, PA 17307.

Websites Connected to Doc Yeager

www.docyeager.com

www.jilmi.org

www.wbntv.org

Made in the USA
Columbia, SC
18 September 2020

21012546R00041